C000089893

PARADOXICAL VISTA

Copyright © 2020
All Rights Reserved

www.paradoxicalvista.org

Love Poems

FROM THE UNIVERSE

By D. J. Irvine

Love is born in the stars.

Dedicated to Josephine O'toole.

Thanks for all the loving stories you've shared.

CONTENTS

If beauty is born from the stars

If beauty is born from the stars
A galaxy must fracture & embark
Because love holds gravity together
Making all life a work of art.

We found each other on this journey of scars
Defining our purpose in each other's arms
Talking about fate like it was lost
Near an old wooden gate –
That was made for us to kiss on
Of this day of dark-less quasars.

We laughed & planned our life together
Picking out crafts & mastery bazaars
It was like we were superstars
Dancing on the sands of Mars.

Our time on this line was delivered
Almost like it was written
Falling in love again
Like it was the first time
In a place designed for the innocent.

& with that we made a decision…
We would never let go of our position
But create children & thank the universe
For all that it's humbly given.

Tears of
salt

Her tears filled up the universe
Leaving behind puddles of salt
That can now be seen as meteors
Speeding through space
Between galactical faults.

Tears that carry all the designs
Tears built for another time
Tears shed as an old world
Was swallowed by fate
On this journey defined by someone
Holding the keys to a dark blank slate.

Salted tears cried by both Women & Men
Made to start the process again
For a lost love
Forgotten,
As light becomes rotten.

She left behind life
To begin again
Across the dark matter,
Sifting through this infinite place.

Bouncing through the centre of black holes
Built to store love
In an orange & pink lagoon
Held together by gravity's pull.

Will we meet again?

As strangers, we both turned
& like a quasar from a black hole
We fell into each other's eyes
Dancing like a nebula from a garden rose.

We smiled,
We traded moments of lost soul.
No words were exchanged
In this infinite moment of poetic hold.

& with that
We departed
Never to know,
Why our magnetic pull
Decided to reverse.

Dancing with the sea

Her silhouette glows in the moonlight
As she dances with the waves of the sea.
Crashing between her feet
Like bubbling champagne -
Kissing garnet strawberries
Beneath the dark of the breeze.

The moist billion-year-old grains of sand
Hold her hand
Guiding her home,
To dry land.

Dancing with the sea
Has tired her perfect form.
As she looks for footprints
Left by her own.

Waiting for her man

The warmth from her slender neck
Caresses the silky soft waves of the duvet set,
Slipped over her naked body
Wrapped up like a present for sex.

A love note was left,
After the night spent
Which read...

This love can never end.
Xx

Pain of love

Shelter me from the pain of love
A hurt that cannot be measured
Especially if the laws of the universe
Demand it be undone.

She has no scars,
She needs no wings,
She bleeds like an angel crying for her sins.

She weeps for her feelings
& looses them in the rain.
She's dead in the morning until she
Drinks the golden liquid
That can leave a nasty stain.
She waits, she commands, she's ready with her plan.
She delivers new children into the world
Without a helping hand.

We stand & stare & wonder how they can,
Who are we?
Just a simple man.

She carries

life

Moonlight

She hid her smile
In the glow of moonlight.

Whispered

I felt her breath on my ear
As she whispered something
I'll never forget.

Our engagement
was a prophecy

We found each other by chance
Like magic, we formed an exclusive path.
Together, like a universal dance
Built beyond our imagination
From an innocent glance.

If dreams could talk,
If dreams could walk,
If dreams could ignite the illusion of thought.

We would emerge presenting rings together
Defining this reality of infinite art.

The day we met
Time stood still,
Until we sealed a bond
Like it was written in a story before we were gone.

It all made sense,
It all felt right,
It all stood for something...
In these moments of living delights.

The spark of our smiles,
The stares lasted for miles,
The pools of shallow breath –
Imprisoned our love to the death.

While we twisted time & gravity together
So the divine could spectate from above.

We knew,
Without a given clue
That our engagement was to be true,
As our love for each other grew
& grew.

The gaze she held

Her gaze hides from reality
Because she is here
But her soul was not.

She has the ability to look straight through beings
While defining the sense of seeing
As she keys her energy into this moment of bleeding.

She gazed upon reality as the world watched,
She was here but she couldn't touch.

You meet them, you see them
You ponder on their dreams.

Because so few have the ability of a gaze
That breaks existence
For all that it's got.

Timeless

We met again at the bus station.
& held hands as 20 years
Drove past.

Our secret

We make love in the shadows,
Kiss in secret
& cuddle under the apple blossom.

The dream

we made

We painted pictures in the stars,
Gazing beyond a journey
That will never be ours.
But we dreamed about it anyway
& longed to be in each other's arms.

For the dreams were all we had
As we made love between the Moon & Mars.

The universe watched
Placing memories that will never be forgot,
As we looked upon each other
& the future joined the dots.

But we chanced upon our dreams
& spent time going to extremes.
Without the need for screams
In the lightness of our esteems.

Until one day we spoke about
How the years had slowly past,
With all the time that was simply ours,
Completed with all those simple tasks.

The dream we made
From a distant past.
We made it
& that was all we really asked.

Show
love

Kiss her goodbye,
Even when the kids are close by.

Fly without wings

Embrace her swings,
Care for his moods
& fly without wings for each other.

Her starlight
& dreams

She wept under her dying star
For it had given life to all it could touch.
A moment lost under the red & blue dust
That can now be seen as a nebula,
From a distance that can never be touched.

Her starlight & dreams dissipate
Into the black expanse,
Becoming stardust
To create new moments of chance.

All the love in the universe
Couldn't stop the outburst
Of the perishing star,
That completes the sequence
Like the death of Mars.

Just like beautiful dreams
All must come to an end.
Balancing on the strings of gravity
To produce a meaningful descend.

Her tears filled with fantasy
Froze with fire & pansophy,
As she flew off to another galaxy
To give birth until the end.

& that's when he awoke!
Transcending from the layers of broken smoke
With a realisation of the damage
Put out by an uncontained choke.

So, he followed her into the distant stars
Because he wanted to be that end
But this time – without time,
A realm built for the divine.

We

walked

We walked between the valleys
We walked over the hills
We felt the lush of the soft butterflies –
Dancing through the azure skies,
All while falling in love with each other's eyes.

We walked through the cerulean meadows
We walked into the lost fields,
Hidden between the chattering ghetto's
We could smell the fresh air
That fell into our love drenched lungs.

We danced
We ran
We fed each other words of wisdom
Made up by our delicate tongues.

We held hands & spoke about our Mum's
We kissed for a moment
Under the dying tangerine sun,
We remembered the time
When life was just intoxicating fun.

We walked until it was dark
We walked through the children singing in the park,
We walked until our feet began to perish
On the stones that filled the floor & the heavens.

We laughed
We smiled
We hustled through the cornfields
Sneezing pollen back into the lands.

We made it home
We put logs on the fire
We were silent but listened
To the crack of the seasoned wood
While sipping red wine
In a time that we could.

Laugh

We both laugh with each other
& that's why it works.

Follow

her

She would walk for miles,
Talking about all the things she wanted to do.
I would follow her
& follow her
& follow her.

Cosmos

Her tears filled the cosmos
With stardust.

My
dreams

I smiled
I told her my dreams
Because no one else would listen like her.

Pretended

We pretended to be married
& loved each other anyway.

Burst banks

When she cried the rain came.
Her tears spilt across the river lane.
Sometimes the banks burst
& love was at its very worst.

Live life

She never wore black
& we never went to any funerals,
Because life is to live.

World of pain

The whisky made him stink of shame,
She held him & embraced his sane.
A woman of sorrow & took the blame,
As her man was lost to a world of pain.

Pink gin & whisky

She drank pink gin, whisky & lemonade
He drunk pink gin, whisky & Indian tonic
As the world turned,
To twist light into a dark adonic.

We see galaxies colliding
As we peer into these glasses of nebula
With the lemon & lime flavour of zest
Bringing us towards another quest.

This moment creates a living chime
Just past the event horizon
That bends the fabric of space-time
Spilling gin & whisky on ice
To make a drink that was made to entice.

We remember the times when we had no means
As the starlight offers up new dreams.

We drink to love
We drink to time
We drink to a partnership
Like pink gin & whiskey
Was born to make this climb.

Over ice...
2 shots of pink gin
1 shot of single grain Scotch whisky
2 slices of fresh lemon
1 slice of fresh lime
1 small bottle of Indian tonic water (sparkling)
Or lemonade.

Impossible

We lost love
But found it again,
Surrounded by impossible circumstances.

Out out

We were out out
& realized we weren't missing much.

The universal code

of love

There is a universal code of love
Hidden deep & remains untouched.
To find it you must discover trust
In the valley filled with diamonds & dust.

Love stretches through the curvature of space
Reaching all beings of a different race.
Because all the galaxies are connected
With energy defined by a memory of place.

The colour of love can be found in a dying star.
Sometimes it can be seen in a comet,
Seeking its way to a different Earth.

Love is the torment of a swinging solar system
Bound by gravity on a mystic cataclysm.

The universe commands love
In the palm of its lilliputian hand.
Where life holds the secret in the eyes of its mind.

Love without life
Life without love…

Would create a paradox of existence
That wouldn't be worth living,
As the greens of the grass
Would look colourless & bland.

Love is an entity that captures the breeze
As you kiss on the beach
With your toes sinking in the sand.
Love is tiny like a precious baby's hand
Living out its existence in the light of this plan.

Love is you
Love is me
Love is us
For a moment
In diamonds & dust.

Heart beats
of love

Her heart pumps with desire
Her heart beats like it's on fire
She pounds for his touch
Anticipating his love
As she waits for him
While standing for the shuttle bus.

He sees her long black hair
From a distant stare
With people rushing & bumping with despair…
While disturbing the gap between the path & air.

He composes the conversation in his head
Before he meets her
Between the road & glass shed.

As time shakes both realities hand
A connection begins to unravel the plan
Smiles & heartbeats compose a song
As words form a sentence
Play out for too long.

She feels the rush of blood to her neck
He sees her breath quicken
As the love inside his blood thickens.

Where will this journey end?
A picture worth painting
That was written
Before they became friends.

Old

Love grows
As life gets old.

Hope

Her beauty lit the world with hope,
He built the world so she could cope.

Proposal of love

I proposed on one knee
After you spent the third year with me
Under the apple tree
Where you promised your love for thee.

We spoke of a little house
With an open cracking fire stove
& whispered of children
As we made love
On the black leather couch.

We fell into each other's arms
Eating scones made by nan
We got married in the church
Near that old farmhouse
As we danced & made a million more plans

You fell pregnant with our first little charm
& that's why with 20 years of great
I stand by your side & wait
For you to smile & give me a little kiss at the gate.

Our love grows wild as we drink red wine
We talk about all the little stories we made
Our children are doing great
Which was hard work & kept us up late
But we held love together
For a moment to commemorate.

So, I give you these words
Without any debate...

I couldn't imagine life
Without the love you create.

Free

love

We give each other our love for free,
Unconditionally!
As the air is to breathe in the light of the breeze.
Can you feel our magnetised energy –
Positive & negative?
As our cold skin touches & warms-up,
When we ignite from our journey of free love.

Free us from our chemistry of oxygen & hydrogen,
As our blue blood turns red from the nitrogen.

We cut open our death sentence here on this end.
We give each other our love for free on this mend,
Like life is to happiness without the need to pretend.

Hold me as I hold you,
Cry vivid tears of fantasy
Onto my earned weekend.

Whisper your make believe dreams,
Into the salt of my drying tears.

I want to feel the vibrations of your sweat,
Dripping through my veins
Like on the day we met.

We give each other our love for free.
Just like the sky dances with the sea,
In a time where elephants bleed under the trees.

Do you remember our first kiss in the club?
Where hundreds of people danced in the dust.

Our love was for free,
Like life was given to us –
In a moment of trust,
Before the magic of lust...

We were both born to meet in a crack,
That formed actuality –
As the floods moved across the green lands
& left behind bronze mud statue's of mortality.

Give up your local fame in the name of love.
Leave behind old lusts of shame & start again,
With all that endless game.

Our love is for free –
Free is our love.

Remember, that flying white dove
Is made of gold,
In the rising sun from above.

Poets

We kissed like poets,
Breathing words
That will never be heard.

Magic tricks

We showed each other our magic tricks,
But still kept them a secret.

When love
is lost

Somewhere through the window of time,
We forgot about the moments
That led to our loving climb.
We grew through the ages of each other's skin
While twisting through life,
Like a tornado in a spin.

Somewhere we lost love
Love that bound us to start & begin.
A feeling that brings tears & joy
Through the eye of a needle while sipping pink gin.

We tore ourselves apart
Like a galaxy from a distant past
Living life with all its asks
Helping us make a new start.

Love defines our living tasks
Of partnership bound by a smiling mask.
Now time has become your friend
Until the long-term memories start to descend.

Love will find us again
Love will start time again.
Love waits until we reach for the clouds
Like in that dream
Between the darkness of the shroud.

Smile & show the pearls of our teeth
Breath & let the blood rush through our feet.

Because of love,
We feel the hurt & pain
While softly listening to our heartbeat
Living life from the beginning again.

The enchantment of a softly spoken midwife

She wore a delicate smile
She adored all things wild
She loved his flavour
She thanked his maker
That he simply wasn't an opinionated faker.

He wore muscles with a frown of course
He adored all things delicate
But designed with force
He loved her olive skin as they both drunk gin
In the ambience of the pink skies –
Distorted within.

He thanked her brown glowing eyes
For all the moments of surprise
She smiled at him in the morning wind
Beyond where the mountain stands still.

The bond of love grew with these two souls
Wrapping the simplicity of time & gravity
Making sure that all perceived reality
Combined by the making of actuality.

They passed on this love
To everyone they touched
Including their children,
For their appreciation was a must.

& that's where they discovered
The secret to life
A moment caught by chance & surprise

In the enchantment of a softly spoken midwife.

In the mornings

She wanted to make love in the mornings;
Under the starlight
From the sun.

Wild

He was wild & she wanted to tame him.

She smiled & he was drunk in love.

The pact

we made

We made a pact
From this life to the next
As we lay here naked on this tired old bed.

We forgot about love
A word we never used
Just that look
Was good enough.

Life seemed all wrapped up
Beyond that first place
Where the London train pulled up.

Our captured smiles reflected
In the solid grey platform
That only we could see
Because love just wasn't enough
A word that couldn't set us free.

Turning & twisting like a perfected dance
We raced through life
Like it was written by chance.

The days & nights were built on romance
As the universe collided galaxies together
For two people lost in each others trance.

We made a pact
With no words of exchange
As our souls grow old together
On this tired old frame.

For all our memories are the same
& that's why we still smile with no shame...

We were meant to be
As we lay here naked
On this old tired bed frame.

A story built for you & me.

Maybe we wrote it together
Just before we came
Because where we come from
This only pretend.

Drunk &

Sober

She was drunk on orgasmic tinglings.
He was sober
From the fumes
Of her vanilla perfume.

Found

her

She was lost in life
But he found her
Before it was too late.

Time to
meet love

We wait for each other's presence;
Deciphering the time
Like a bottle of aged essence.
Composing a gentle touch
Beyond the fragmented moments of such.

The seconds on a clock,
Slow & almost stop
As we talk under the dying stars
& awaken memories imprisoned on Neptune.

Combining the messages of new,
Outdoing all the notes that compose me & you.
Is this real?
Or a twisted fragmentation
Of physical manipulation.

We kiss into a transfixed osculation
While our exhalation turns into animation.

Travelling between the layers of consciousness,
Igniting chemistry;
Enabling us to fall into a state of tranquillity.

We collide
Like the dark meeting particles of luminosity.

The seconds speed up,
As reality
Catches love.

We lost
love

You said you wanted happiness
You said you wanted nothing else
We created beings together
& watched laughter echo
Through the vibrations of life itself.

We did all this in the name of love
Standing by each other
As time moved on.

We had it all
Yet we had nothing
We had each other
With feelings made to dance for one another.

& then one day you left
& danced with another
Who gave you no rest
As I walked home in a mess.

& I watched
& fell to dust
As I lost you forever
In the darkness
& the glow of Saturn
In the clouds from above.

Spilt tears

He wrote her a love letter
& she spilt tears,
Until the words disappeared.

Ignited

He said hello with a beautiful smile,
& her soul ignited to become his fate.

The black hole
of love

The centre of the black hole stopped
As we met for the first time on this rock.
Creating a ripple of love
That interlinked gravity.
To break the laws of actuality.
Pulling us closer –
To ignite the universe
On this infinite moment of magnificent ride.

We smiled
Because we both knew,
That a moment escaped from the galaxy
Creating the energy for normality
Which can only be played out in this reality
Had fractured for the first time.

& so the journey began
Without hesitation of this plan
A partnership pulled together
Of a place, we can't measure
But here to feel pleasure
Of why love
Holds the universe together
Until
The
End
Of
Time.

I've found
a place

It's all me
It's all you
I've found a place
Where we can make love all night.

Together, forever
Until the end of time
A place where we can smile & feel divine.

I'll meet you there at half past nine
I'll be ready
With red & white wine
Forever, we can extract each other's mind.

We can start with a little kiss
& penetrate each other's breath

Like the wind
When it blows out the night.

It's all you
It's all me
I've found a place
Where we can make love all the time.

I want this love to last forever
Like the universe
Entwined with a multi-dimensional rhyme
A chance to create life itself
With a girl who has no time.

I'll meet you there at half past nine
I'll be ready
With red & white wine
Forever, we can extract each other's mind.

& all this time
We spent years looking for a place
That was right in front of our face
As we laughed together
When the clock tower chimed.

White

dove

She wrote the words
While feeling love.
He read them
& found a delicate white dove.

The thing
about love

She wanted it to last forever

So he carried on

& on

& on.

The moon

watches

The moonlight designed her silhouette –
Hovering across the landscape
Of pongee bedsheets
As the gentle silvery light glistened
From a thousand miles away
Anticipating the movement from her presence
Creating shadows
Like naked mannequins.

She looked beyond the ball of crystal fire
& caught the light from scintillating stars
As she reached over to grab the ivory pillow
Holding her eyes tightly closed
From the electric sensation of penetration.

She reached the apex of climax
Naked,
Nipples pert
Letting her warm breath do the work
While endorphins saturated her inner universe.

The achromatic moon watches on
Collecting memories from billions of silhouettes
Dancing out the illusion of different songs.

Love is a smile

Love, they said with a smile
& a smile they said with love
Because if you listen closely
A smile is born out of love.

Can you hear the love?
Can you see love?
Can you feel the love?

Love entangles itself around your spine
Making life believable & sometimes kind.

Love is the most idolized word of its time.

Lost in love

I'm lost in life finding the one
She never comes to me when I'm looking for fun
I await in the pub
I await in the club
Sometimes, I make conversation for no reason,
Like a chump.

Maybe it's best to stay in
Let me create an account & log in
But that's just not me
Pretending behind a computer screen.

So, I know I must
Hunt for her over all these lands
Around the globe
Awaiting to take her hand...

Dancing between the glow of the stars

She flew in her ship between the stars
From a future that I can't ask
Because if I do
I might miss her
When she laughs at my deluded plans.

She wants to be a rock-n-roller
Just for one afternoon
In the shed
When I turn up the volume to way past ten.

She dresses in a material I've never seen
Which cleans itself & creates a new theme.

She looks into my lazy eye
& plants visions of never to be seen.

& then she leaves
Promising to return in my dreams.

It was

written

She wanted fame without no shame
She wore to kill
She walked to bend eyes – outside in
She knew her power
She sought to win! Without playing in this game.

She could swim
She went to the gym
You had to be free to see her grin.

She would approach you
With her wild blue & green eyes.

Looking through you
Like a spider's web in disguise.

For all that was you
She understood your mood
But you had to follow her on the road
That was written where she stood.

One more

time

Let's lay down the hard times
Let's play for the times that we want to come true
Let's do it together for our children & our mother's too.

We can do it, I know if we try
Forget about the past – a moment left to dry.
Defeat!
Does not exist
When we work together & make this it!

I can see the sparkle & flash in your frozen eyes
When I smile & tap you on the bum,
& kiss you on the neck – leaving my innocent scent.

Let's try one more time
Let's not break the marriage photo
I can't live on my own again.

Softly breathing her breath

Slowly kissing her neck
She whispers sweet somethings
Beyond my fragmented intellect.
Softly breathing her breath,
Swallowing her sweat,
Never to regret
As she watches my hands
Move around her enticing breasts.

Her skin-tight jeans
Wrapped around her cheeks
Like an infested disease,
Not letting her skin breath.

Unravel with ease
Revealing her slight legs,
Beautiful feet,
& lingerie –
Wrapped up like a gift set.

She waits for it
To enter her wet,
Tight,
For a moment
Before shuddering
On the soft silver bed sheets.

She smiles & watches
With all intent.
Then we laugh together
As life was meant.

Into the night
with delight

Dancing into the damp fog of the night
Twisting & turning through the distorted norms of delight
Feeling frightened when awakening from the sight
Of a construed shadow lurking
Within the cracked bricks
Of the shop window with no light.

Vanished from the night
Like catching a black cats shadow
Twisting with delight
Never to catch sight
As a car passes offering bright white light.

Dirty bare feet from the old cobbled streets
Caressing an empty market square in the night
Perfect toes that fit the carried red stilettos
Of a stranger who is feeling delight.

A journey that starts to pretend
As the time is lost in the night
Emotions heightened
Offering chemical reactions of delight
Touching & kissing with blinded sight
As the dark turns into a moment of light.

Night turning into day
Delight fading into regret
Sight blinded with the toxicities
Of a self-conflicted mess
Light blankets kicked off with a pounding head.

One journey that comes to an end.

Tink

Tink, you are the twinkle in my eye
You make me feel alive
Like a twilight in the sky.

As the world moves around us
Our love grows like a rose.

You are my fire
My desire
The true love of my chose.

I fell in love

once

I didn't even see her,
Until one day I felt her stare
Across my back
Like a warm summers day
With a blossom of scent in the air.

I turned to catch a glimpse
& saw a woman that was looking for her prince.

After several exchanges of glare,
I noticed a woman so rare
Something came over me
That I can not explain
A feeling that didn't leave me
For an eternal flame.

Her eyes were golden brown
Like the reflection of a Queen's crown,
Black hair that set fire to her shy stare
Olive skin that looked perfect
When she went into the water to swim.

Felt her before seeing her
Our eyes would meet on the other side of the street
A look that exchanged a thousand words,
Yet a delivery of feeling
No words can complete.

She tried to work me out
As one day we exchanged words while working out.
I lost her in my verbal muster of cluster
She shook her head in a moment of fluster
To which our magnetic pull reversed.

The path parted into a different time
It wasn't to be on this line
As the bells chimed for a different mind.

I won't see her again,
Not in this time.

Sleeping lady

Breathing softly
Pink dry lips await a wet lick
From her lavishing tongue.

Eyes moving sharply, twisting & dancing
As her mind unravels the days
Of events that can't be undone.

Strands of hair so perfectly combed
Before she lay undressed
In the safety of her home.

One hand under the cloudy white pillow
As the other couples her smooth prudent breast.

She mutters a word that sounds familiar
Dreaming away as reality becomes unfamiliar.

She turns & changes position
Without permission
Her body numb,
To the sound of my deluded patterns
Of thinking.

Will she awake to see my yawn?

She's already gone...

I turn the light off & join her on this journey
To a future I saw before we arrived
In this moment of encapsulating some.

Ditto

She doesn't wear makeup

& neither do I.

Out of sight

We sent text messages into the night,
So those words would always stay out of sight.

Torn open

Like magic,
We disappeared
& got drunk on memories
Torn open by the years.

Sober on

poetry

She was sober on poetry
Gazing into the heavens - knowingly.

The journey
of a love story

Let me take you on a journey –
Beyond where the sun sets,
Creating a marble golden breeze.
See behind the aperture of the sky,
Touching the darkness of space
Where the blackness of your pupil hides.
Reach out with your mind & let your third eye radiate
Into this distant time.

As long as you look, love will find a way to be kind
While unravelling the edges of realities climb.
He will find you
& she will find you!
On an odyssey that makes love entwine.
Beneath and between the curvature of this dream,
Emotion gives armour for all the unseen.

Breathing enchantment into each other ears –
Brings allegiance to love for all these new years.
Walk with each other while others play that song,
Dance in the shallow water where nothing can go wrong.
Break for the valley and run for the thrills
Because love makes life so strong.

Enjoy the adventure that brings laughs and hate,
& fills up a plate with tears that create.

Roam through the bark filled woods
& watch the deer stand and run from your room.

Venture upon the moon in the lake,
While holding a candle for no given sake.

Breathe the frosty morning into your souls
While fire burns at your toes.

Seek a quest that finds memories
More expensive than gold.
Do it all & do it together
As love offers the fabric for a voyage to be told.

Mortals & the divine

She bled a single tear for
Humanity
Because in the eyes of the
Divine
Mortals lost the war with
Themselves.

She

awaits

The intrusion from her matt pink lips
Intoxicate weak minds
Looking to find a way in.

She smiles to soften the rejection
Of lonely men pretending
As they offer the world
With empty leather wallets
Filled with plastic pearls.

Love was on the agenda
To which she had already chosen
Something that can not be broken
By men who offer silver tokens.

She awaits, in her toxic white dress
For one man to enter
From beyond the streets
With pubs and clubs a mess.

Her perfume captures his breath
As they walk to meet each other
Like celebrity guests
A beautiful married couple –
No less.

Black holes

I fell in love
with the
black holes
inside her
eyes.

What does love mean?

1. Open up to your partner &
express everything you know.
This shows a willingness to interact
& be more open about any situation.

2. Love is but a connection of total comfort.

3. Love can be a simple look of acceptance.

4. Love is when you're at home with your partner
& you find yourself looking for each other.
You can't explain why you do this,
but it's a feeling of being complete.

5. Love is a coupling amalgamation
of satisfaction & achievement.

6. Sometimes a situation can arise
when one will cheat on another.
When confronted with this fact,
love can bring you closer
as it draws on unrealised
emotional states.

7. Love is learned through passion,
lust & physical contact.
Love ends up as a matrix of peace,
compassion & acceptance.

8. Love draws on many emotions,
this is why it's hard to define.
Sometimes a person thinks they don't
know what love is,
until that something is lost.

9. As a child, you love your parents with all your heart.
This love stays with you as an adult
& becomes stronger for your children.
This is the endless family cycle of love.

10. Love can sometimes be found
in a dark place of depression,
stress, ignorance & no self-respect.
Love is hard to let go of
especially, when you haven't found it
with another who draws down
on the kinder sides of love.

11. Love in its own right
is a powerful source of manipulation & passion.
Knowledge of such capacity
can bring danger in many forms.

12. Love can be confusing,
so be patient,
you are here for a long time.

13. Offer your love to ones you know love you.
To be rejected in love is a complex -
emotional feeling of great discomfort.
These feelings will pass but can last a while.

14. When love is broken
it requires you to be brave.
Stand up, take control & focus on your confidence.
Love is behind many corners.

15. To develop a higher understanding of love,
know that love brings with it moments of joy,
laughter & endless amounts of entertainment.

16. Love supplies balance in a relationship.
Even though one may dominate another
with knowledge,
physical presence,
articulation or communication.
Love bonds a couple as one
& projects an ease of ambience.

17. Love through age can fall away
into a place of lost thought.
Concentrate on what you like about your partner.
Ask yourself the question –
why did we fall in love?

18. Love can be described as

warm

sensual

soft

receptive

flourishing

sophisticated

& emotional.

Work on love

& it will bring you moments

of speechless thought.

19. If someone loves you

& you love someone.

You know what they are feeling

because you feel that same thing.

To know this will make you smile,

so cherish your love binding passion

for one another.

20. Love is a text message,

a phone call

or an email,

asking the simple question...

What are you up to?

It's not the question or the action,

but the thought that inspires you

to make it happen.

10 simple ways to fall in love again

1. CHANGE YOUR ROUTINE

Try & get out of that same old routine. Shopping on Saturday, sex once a week or month, moaning about things that never really mattered, sitting in front of the television every night, never going out, arguing over who's turn it is to do a particular job. Compare this to when you first met.

Try & do something different every week. Work as a team & plan a good weekend together. Plot a night of passion that will set you both on fire. The key is to surprise each other, keep each other on your toes & work together. If you do this for each other, it can make the daily routine a more pleasurable experience.

2. COMPLIMENTS

When was the last time you complimented each other? A compliment can go a long way. A simple, "you're looking lovely today", or "I like that dress or shirt on you". Can give a sense of lost pulsating magic & make you feel young again.

3. ROMANCE

Be romantic & go out for a meal. Remember, when you first met, you both had many meals together & enjoyed a bottle of wine. A candlelit dinner makes you feel wanted & warm inside. A simple gesture of calm conversation, whilst enjoying each other's company goes a long way. Send her unexpected flowers with a little note saying how much you love her. Buy each other a simple gift or something nice that will be appreciated. Why not send her a beautiful love poem & slip it into her handbag.

4. TOUCH EACH OTHER

Offer your partner a relaxing massage & really spend time with each other, caressing & easing all those worries & stressful days away. Normally a few candles can increase the mood & the scent from the burning wax can be really tranquil.

5. A BATH

Run your partner a hot bath for when they return home from work, make sure you put plenty of bubbles in. This can be surprising & there is nothing like the pleasures of a hot bath for a soothing 30-minute soak.

6. CONVERSATION

Listen to each other & ask questions about each other's day. Don't sit there & pretend. There is nothing worse than knowing that your partner is not taking any notice of your words of conversations.

7. GET FAMILY ORIENTATED

Play with the kids & spend a couple of hours a week doing something together. Board games, walks around the park, talk time, cards, gardening & keeping fit. Never sit around the house looking at each other, complaining you can't afford to do anything.

8. TEXT

Try & send each other a sexy text message every now & again. Make an effort & find that connection. If you can't communicate face-to-face & probably start laughing at each other, then a text message is a great way of expressing yourself, without finding the situation embarrassing.

9. HOBBY

Find something to do in your spare time. There is so much to do if you look. Sit down & give each other a piece of blank paper. Now both write down what you would like to do. Compare your notes & get involved. Dancing, rock climbing, fishing, wrestling, water sports, painting, orienteering, bird watching & photography are a few ideas to get you started.

10. ACTIVITIES

Get out of the house with the whole family. Visit a castle or a huge adventure park. If you check with the local library you will find plenty to do in your area. A family day out is one of the most pleasant experiences of being a proud parent.

Book

dedications

I have to dedicate this book to my loving Nan - Josephine O'toole. Her laughs, stories, jokes and dedication to me and my brother (Stephen) were unstoppable. I couldn't even imagine where I would be in life without her guidance, sharp eye for detail and the wisdom she passed on to me. She fell asleep into the darkness many years ago, however, her youthful presence will stay with me forever.

From an early age I would pop round to see her. She gave me jobs to do around the house, had me doing shift work in the garden and sent me to the shops for all her groceries. She trusted me and I loved her for that.

She would tell me her life stories and she knew the answers to every question I had. If I ever said "I just can't do it Nan" she would give me a fierce look from her light blue eyes and tell me "There's no such thing as can't". She was bloody right!

I wrote this book and the next poem for a wonderful woman - who directed me on the right path.

There's no such thing as can't!

A teacher, a philosopher, a talker of all
Full of wisdom for even more,
Untouchable, with a mind that can do!
Is this real?
This person of overwhelming chore.

Stories of old, history to be told
Excitement, smiles and everlasting hold.

Passing on
Everything needed for a new journey to be told.
"Tell me again"
Get the job done & don't pretend.
Talking me through the jobs to be done
Hoovering - Polishing - Dishes - Gardening
Shopping - Reading & Pop to the shops
All while singing a merry song.

"I can't do it"
Trying to pretend.

She pointed the finger and glared again
"There's no such thing as can't"
She would repent.

A life lesson learnt until the very end.

Passing on the message still
Through my eyes the letter spent
As my children spill
A defiant dent.

Unknowing until time is old
A paradox the future holds.

A beautiful poetic woman
My Nan
Josephine O'Toole.

To

Tink

What would a book about 'love poems' be like without a page dedicated to my beautiful wife? I don't know, so here goes; To my wife Emma Irvine (Tink). Thanks for all the wonderful years together, thanks for our 4 handsome Sons (No more children now please!) and thanks for all the laughs and memories we have built together. Here is another poem just for you and all the readers to peer into.

My Wife

My wife puts things into perspective!
Even when I'm right or wrong – irrespective.
She commands the children with her song,
And I listen, pretending not to see her yawn.

She cooks me a three-course meal,
With white wine and homemade scones.
I offer her an ear for conversation
While she talks about all life's wrongs.

Sometimes, I see her running around the bedroom,
In her silky black thong;
and then she reminds me of why we could –
Never be alone...

I wait for her whenever she's late
I smile when she arrives home late at the gate.
I arise to the occasion, only for her need,
And then she uses me as a sofa –
For her delicate little feet.

We nag at each other
From the corners of the street.
She bleeds white tears
That roll softly down her cheeks.
We laugh together –
Talking about stories of all our family members,
Making a mess,
While we grow old in a moment of stress.

She's my friend,
My lover,
The woman who kisses our children in times of need.

What could any man want more?
If it was only for a moment of greed.

We married in the garden,
Under a sky of wooden beams,
While all our friends and family
Laughed at our Scottish theme.

But now its time to reflect on love,
For this book was penned
Under the stars from above.

We can now look at each other –
Through a galaxy of eyes,
And share this dream
That was born to surprise.

William

I love spending time with all my Sons, especially little William (the last one) who is now 3. There's something special a father has with his young son(s) growing up. As they grow older and become more independent, distant and grow into their own person; you miss the time spent with them growing up. From birth to around 8 years of age, are the very precious years for a father (and mother). This is the time you teach them, talk to them, show them and engage with their busy little schedule of building and developing. They hold your hand and guide you to engage in life, and they remind you to enjoy reality as we know it. I wrote this poem for my youngest Son William; to remind myself how amazing life is when he's by my side.

Walking with my Son

I walk with my little son
He would follow me to the edges of the galaxy
Just to tell me his story of his love for reality.

He waits for my return
Then tells me he misses me
With a smile, a cuddle and kiss
That reminds me he's here in this world.

He gives me tasks to do
While playing in the evening
Then I read him a story
Way past bedtime.

We walk in the morning
While he points out rivers of gold
in the sunrise of the morning cold.

He wears his Wellington boots
That always soak his socks
From the lakes spilling through
The tired broken locks.

We walk in the winter snow
But he never tells me
How his hands look so cold
He steps over the white mountains
And laughs when he falls –
While shouting "Hey, Dad! Did you see that?"

We talk about all those crazy baby things
He reminds me of how life
Is just a push on a swing
We laugh about Mum staying in
Then we talk about his older brothers
Being naughty and doing silly things.

My little boy just turned 3
And does things
That completely amaze me.

He sings all the words to every song
He points at Mum
When she's doing things wrong
He combines his vision
To build a life
Free from a rotten old prison.

But most importantly of all
He gives his love…
Like magic is to a unicorn.

You see,

Love has many stories.

Acknowledgements

If you have read any of my other poetry & wisdom books, you will know I get all my images from unsplash.com There is a great range of beautiful photography to choose from; it's all free to use for creative work. Here's a big thankyou! to all the people that helped me complete this book.

Alejandra Quiroz
Alexander Andrews
Aliyah-jamous
Bryan Goff
Chirag
Christopher Campbell
Cristian Newman
Dan Dealmeida
David Monje
David Cohen
Davide Sibilio
Evren Sydin
Ferdinand Feng
Dan Grinwis
Frank Mckenna
Gaelle Marcel
Gaston Roulstone
Graham Holtshausen
Hisu Lee

Houcine-ncib
Jade
Jasper Boer
Jill Heyer
Jovaughn Stephens
Juskteez Vu
Khadeeja Yasser
Kunj Parekh
Luca Bravo
Maddi Bazzocco
Makenna Entrikin
Marc Wieland
Maru Lombardo
Matthew Hamilto
Mia Harvey
Mohamed Nohassi
NASA
Ricardo Rocha
Roberto Nickson
Sam Schooler
Sean
Simon Migaj
Simon Waelti
Sommi H
Soroush Karimi
Stephen Leonardi
Susanne Feldt
Sylvie Tittel
Szilvia Basso
Taylor Leopold
V2osk
Yoann Boyer

Special thanks

THE EDITOR
A huge thanks goes to Silva Walker for editing this book. She has a sharp eye for detail and her efforts complete this books purpose.

SOCIAL NETWORKING
I would also like to say thanks to all the people who follow me on Instagram and other social media platforms. Your likes and comments are beautiful and inspire me everyday.

PARADOXICALVISTA.ORG
Why not check out the paradoxicalvista.org website. It's packed with poems, articles, merch and more books by D. J. Irvine.

AVAILABLE ON

GET IT ON
Google Play

PARADOXICAL VISTA

Mind Bending Poetry & Wisdom

D. J. IRVINE

DEATH

COMPOSED FROM THE SHADOWS

POEMS

BY

D. J. IRVINE

To Erin & Freya

I hope you enjoy this book

all the best

Printed in Poland
by Amazon Fulfillment
Poland Sp. z o.o., Wrocław

53941640R00090